G000039746

Heroes
of the Revolution

American Cars and Cuban Beats

ear
BOOKS
MINI

Photos by Robert Polidori

Copyright © 2005 by edel CLASSICS GmbH, Hamburg/Germany
All photographs © Robert Polidori
Special-Car-Infos by Helge Thomsen and MB
Music copyright see music credits

ISBN 3-937406-53-0

Designed by Guido Scarabottolo and Raffaela Busia
Adapted for earBOOKS mini by Petra Horn

Produced by optimal media production GmbH, Röbel/Germany
Printed and manufactured in Germany

earBOOKS is a division of edel CLASSICS GmbH
For more information about earBOOKS please browse **www.earbooks.net**

Heroes Of The Revolution
28 x 28 cm
107 photos, 132 pgs.
4 Music CDs
ISBN 3-937406-13-1

Gefällt Ihnen dieses Buch?
Noch mehr Bilder und Musik genießen Sie
im earBOOKS Großformat.

If you liked this book,
you will enjoy the large format earBOOKS
with additional music and pictures.

Si vous avez aimez ce livre, vous l'apprécierez
dans sa version earBOOKS grand format,
avec encore plus de musiques et de photographies.

CD

LOS PASOS PERDIDOS – RITMOS DE CUBA

TRÍO TESIS
Hermes Fernández Salgado: *maracas, percussion, vocals*;
René Mateo Lugos: *guitar, vocals*;
Erasto R. Torres Martínez: *tres, requinto, vocals*;

1 Oye mi son *(son)* 3:46
(Antonio Fernandez Ortiz "Ñico Saquito") Peer International Corp.

2 Ojos malignos (*trova tradicional*) 3:14
(Juan Pichardo Cambié) Editora Musical de Cuba

3 El amor de mi bohío (*guajira*) 3:43
(Julio Brito) Southern Music Publ. Co., Inc.

4 Cuidadito compay gallo (*guaracha*) 2:50
(Antonio Fernandez Ortiz "Ñico Saquito") Egrem Ediciones Musicales

5 Convergencia (*bolero tradicional*) 2:20
(Bienvenido J. Gutiérrez) Egrem Ediciones Musicales

6 Guantanamera (*guajira*) 5:14
(Joseíto Fernández) Quiroga S. L. Ediciones

7 Don Ramón (*son*) 4:02
(Bienvenido Julián Gutiérrez, Rafael Ortiz Rodriguez) Peer International Corp.

8 Tú, mi delirio (*bolero*) 3:51
(César Portillo de la Luz) Peer International Corp.

9 Que manera de quererte (*guaracha*) 4:17
(Luis Emilio Rios Morales) Editora Musical de Cuba

10 Yolanda (*canción*) 4:32
(Pablo Milanés) Autores Produtores Asociados

11 El carretero (*guajira-son*) 2:59
(Guillermo Portabales) Peer International Corp. of Puerto Rico

12 No juegues con mi santo Marilú (*son*) 5:01
(traditional)

13 Hasta siempre comandante (*canción-guajira*) 4:23
(Carlos Manuel Puebla) Egrem Ediciones Musicales

14 Son de la loma (*son*) 5:21
(Miguel Matamoros) Peer International Corp.

A production of Winter & Winter.
Producer: Stefan Winter
Executive Producer: Mariko Takahashi and Stefan Winter
℗ 2002 Winter & Winter, Munich, Germany

PHOTO INDEX

1938 Chevrolet Master

1956 Cadillac

1945 Buick Roadmaster

1953 Chevrolet Coupé

1958 Buick Special

1958 Chevrolet Bel Air

1953 Chevrolet Bel Air

1955 Chevrolet Bel Air

1948 Oldsmobile Dynamic

1955 Oldsmobile Super 88

1955 Plymouth Belvedere Station Wagon
1951 Chevrolet Styleline

1951 Chevrolet Styleline

1949 Buick Special

1946 Chevrolet Stylemaster

1956 Pakkard Clipper

1946 Plymouth Special

1946 Dodge Custom
1956 Plymouth Belvedere

1949 Buick Sedanet

1948 Chevrolet Fleetline
1950 Chevrolet Styleline

1953 Plymouth Cambridge

1958 Chevrolet Bel Air
1958 Chrysler Windsor

1954 Chevrolet Bel Air

1953 Buick Roadmaster

1946 Plymouth Special

1953 Chevrolet Deluxe

1957 Oldsmobile Super 88

1953 Chevrolet Deluxe

1959 Chevrolet Bel Air

1946 Chevrolet Aerosedan

1959 Desoto Adventurer

1948 Chevrolet Fleetline

1960 Chevrolet Impala

1958 Chevrolet Bel Air
1937 Pontiac Deluxe

1947 Chevrolet Sedan
1958 Plymouth Fury

1949 Buick Super Sedanet

1953 Chevrolet
1950 Buick Roadmaster

1953 Chevrolet Bel Air

1959 Chevrolet Impala

1929 Ford "A" modified

Editorial note:
Because many cars on the Cuban island have been modified by their owners
over many years, we were not able to precise the exact specifications of each
car that is shown in the photographs. If you are able to provide us with more
detailed information, we would be very grateful. Please contact us via email:
earbooks@edel.com

Many thanks for your help!
The edel Classics team